George Washington's
MOUNT VERNON

Colonial Williamsburg

**NATIONAL
GEOGRAPHIC**

WASHINGTON, D.C.

How to sit, stand, smile, & Be Cool!

George Washington's

ules

.TO LIVE BY

A GOOD MANNERS GUIDE

FROM THE FATHER OF OUR COUNTRY

K. M. KOSTYAL

ILLUSTRATED BY FRED HARPER

FOREWORD BY LIZZIE POST, THE EMILY POST INSTITUTE

To my son, Will
—KMK

Published by the National Geographic Society
John M. Fahey,
    Chairman of the Board and Chief Executive Officer
Declan Moore,
    Executive Vice President; President, Publishing and Travel
Melina Gerosa Bellows,
    Executive Vice President; Chief Creative Officer,
    Books, Kids, and Family

Prepared by the Books Division
Hector Sierra,
    Senior Vice President and General Manager
Nancy Laties Feresten,
    Senior Vice President, Kids Publishing and Media
Jay Sumner,
    Director of Photography, Children's Publishing
Jennifer Emmett,
    Vice President, Editorial Director, Children's Books
Eva Absher-Schantz,
    Design Director, Kids Publishing and Media
R. Gary Colbert,
    Production Director
Jennifer A. Thornton,
    Director of Managing Editorial

Staff for This Book
Kate Olesin, *Project Editor*
David M. Seager, *Art Director*
Lori Epstein, *Senior Photo Editor*
Ariane Szu-Tu, *Editorial Assistant*
Callie Broaddus, *Design Production Assistant*
Grace Hill, *Associate Managing Editor*
Joan Gossett, *Production Editor*
Lewis R. Bassford, *Production Manager*
Susan Borke, *Legal and Business Affairs*
Jennifer Raichek, *Intern*

Production Services
Phillip L. Schlosser, *Senior Vice President*
Chris Brown, *Vice President, NG Book Manufacturing*
George Bounelis, *Vice President, Production Services*
Nicole Elliott, *Manager*
Rachel Faulise, *Manager*
Robert L. Barr, *Manager*
Art Hondros, *Imaging Technician*

The National Geographic Society is one of the
world's largest nonprofit scientific and educational
organizations. Founded in 1888 to "increase and
diffuse geographic knowledge," the Society's mission
is to inspire people to care about the planet. It
reaches more than 400 million people worldwide each
month through its official journal, *National Geographic*,
and other magazines; National Geographic Channel;
television documentaries; music; radio; films;
books; DVDs; maps; exhibitions; live events; school
publishing programs; interactive media; and
merchandise. National Geographic has funded more
than 10,000 scientific research, conservation and
exploration projects and supports an education
program promoting geographic literacy.

For more information, please visit
www.nationalgeographic.com,
call 1-800-NGS LINE (647-5463),
or write to the following address:

National Geographic Society
1145 17th Street N.W.
Washington, D.C. 20036-4688 U.S.A.

Visit us online at
www.nationalgeographic.com/books

For librarians and teachers:
www.ngchildrensbooks.org

More for kids from National Geographic:
kids.nationalgeographic.com

For information about special discounts for bulk
purchases, please contact National Geographic Books
Special Sales: ngspecsales@ngs.org

For rights or permissions inquiries, please contact
National Geographic Books Subsidiary Rights:
ngbookrights@ngs.org

Hardcover ISBN: 978-1-4263-1500-8
Reinforced Library Binding ISBN: 978-1-4263-1501-5

Printed in China
13/CCOS/1

The Colonial Williamsburg Foundation and
Mount Vernon served as research partners on the
text, not the illustrations, for this book to ensure its
historical accuracy and its faithful portrayal of George
Washington. The caricature-style pen-and-ink and
watercolor illustrations are a playful depiction of
the people of this historical era, including deliberate
exaggeration or distortion of clothing styles and the
like, offered in the spirit of fun.

Contents

❦ Foreword ❧

Etiquette, manners, civility… they all boil down to how we treat one another and how we hope to be seen and understood by those around us. Many people say manners are gone, that etiquette no longer exists. I believe they are wrong.

Emily Post, my great-great-grandmother, always said, "When two people come together, and their lives affect one another, you have etiquette." By this definition etiquette is alive every day. However, it is up to us to bring good etiquette into our lives and extend it graciously to those we encounter—whether holding a door for a stranger or sharing with our closest family and friends.

At the Emily Post Institute we base our etiquette advice on the principles of consideration, respect, and honesty. These principles stand the test of time. Manners are the actions that we take in order to convey these principles. It's respectful to greet someone you meet, to let them know you welcome their presence. Today, we do this by smiling, giving a handshake, or a hug. In previous eras, a curtsy or a bow showed respect and welcomed a gentleman or lady's presence. This goes to show that manners have a wonderful habit of changing as the way we live our lives changes, while the underlying principles remain the same.

George Washington certainly never grappled with whether to answer his cell phone in front of a friend or business colleague. He never had to think about whether to offer someone a seat on the subway, or how to politely reply to an email. However, he had to know how to politely handle a messenger bringing news and how to welcome strangers as guests at Mount Vernon. He had to know which side of the street to walk on when escorting his wife around town. He also had to know proper coach etiquette when sharing a ride with others.

While each of these things may be handled differently today, and while many of them are obsolete, the principles of etiquette that drive manners always remain the same: Be considerate and aware of those around you, be respectful of those you encounter, and understand how your actions will either positively or negatively affect them. And always be honest and sincere with your actions. As long as we are sincere with our intentions, even if we make a mistake, others will know we meant no harm or disrespect.

George Washington's Rules to Live By offers a fun and engaging look at how civility, etiquette, and manners were important to one of our nation's most beloved historical figures and how the rules he chose to live by in the 18th century are still worth living by today.

—*Lizzie Post*
The Emily Post Institute

Introduction

Every Action done in Company, ought to be with Some Sign of Respect, to those that are Present.

This means don't disrespect your bros—
whether it's your kid brother, your friend, your
teacher, your mom, or hey, yourself.

We call George Washington
the Father of Our Country, and he's one of the best loved
Americans ever. He had a real knack for inspiring and
leading people, which he did mostly by his example. So
what exactly made him such a great man?

Of course, nobody is really sure how to answer that,
but here's something we do know. When George was
a boy in Virginia, he hand-copied a list called *The
Rules of Civility & Decent Behavior in Company and
Conversation*. The rules were old even in George's day.
They had been written almost 150 years before by French

Jesuits—priests and teachers in the Catholic Church—and passed on from generation to generation. The rules covered just about everything: how to have good table manners; how to respect other people; how to be a good citizen; even how to sit, stand, talk, and what expression to have on your face.

There are 110 of these rules, but some of them are a lot alike, so we've chosen 50 of our favorites for this book. We've also kept the strange spellings, commas, and capital letters just the way George had them. If you'd like to check out the full list, head to page 120. Some of the rules will seem kind of silly now, and they'll probably give you a good laugh. But scholars think that G.W. really took them to heart and decided to live by them.

Things were much stricter back then than they are today. Children were expected to behave like proper little ladies and gentlemen. And that's exactly what George wanted to be—proper. But more than anything else, he wanted to be an honorable man, and the rules were about how to become that. In fact, the first rule, stated opposite, and the last, on page 119, sum up all the rest.

By the final rule, you'll know how to be a proper lady or gentleman yourself—and a very honorable person as well—someone George would admire.

M

What to do and not to do so people will like eating with you

Table Manners

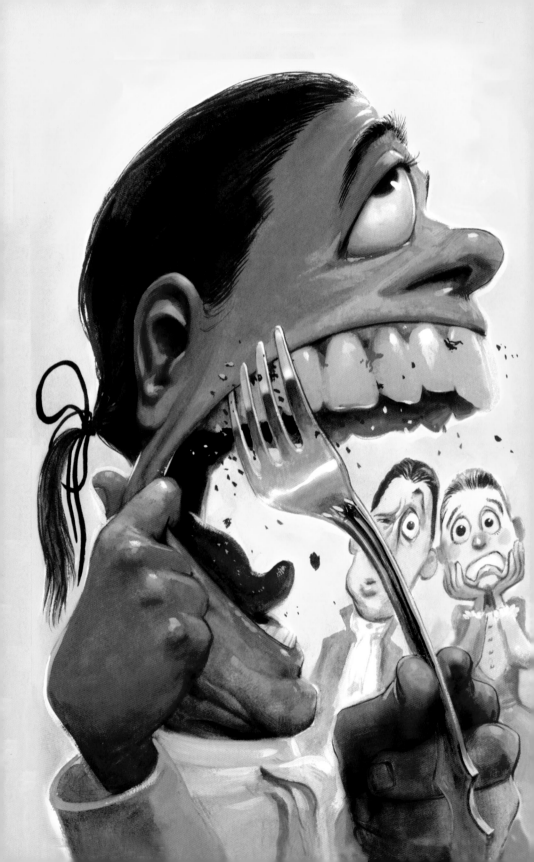

Cleanse not your teeth with the Table Cloth Napkin Fork or Knife but if Others do it let it be done wt. a Pick Tooth.

Gross! Who wants to watch somebody rub their teeth clean with a tablecloth or a napkin, or pick at them with a knife or fork? But back in George's day, toothpickin' was okay, so long as everybody else was doing it, too!

☞ *Poor old George had problems with his teeth. He used all kinds of tooth powders, a silver toothbrush, and a tongue scraper but they must not have worked very well, because he kept losing teeth.*

☞ *When he was inaugurated as the first ever President of the United States, he had only one tooth of his own left, so his dentist made him a set of dentures with a hole for that tooth.*

☞ *You may have heard George wore wooden dentures. Wrong! His dentures were made of ivory from hippopotamus tusk, as well as human teeth, brass, and other weird stuff.*

Make no Shew of taking great Delight in your Victuals, Feed not with Greediness . . .

Nobody likes a sloppy, slurpy eater, right?
Or somebody who's picky about what they eat
and complains about everything.

☞ *George may have had good manners, but he definitely liked to eat. Here's what he and his wife, Martha, had for breakfast one morning, according to a visiting friend: "Mrs. Washington herself made tea and coffee for us. On the table were two small plates of sliced tongue, dry toast, bread and butter, but no broiled fish" (which they usually ate).*

☞ *That's right—tongue! Tongue was considered a special dish and saved for company. Usually G.W. and Martha had something simple for breakfast. George looooved hoecakes, or corn pancakes, "swimming in butter and honey."*

Eat not in the Streets,
nor in the House,
out of Season.

In George's day, "out of season" didn't mean
what you'd think. It meant snacking between
meals instead of eating at proper mealtimes.

☞ *Back then, people did eat mostly fresh local foods that were in season,
because there were no freezers to store food for a long time. Rich people
had icehouses, though—big, roofed holes in the ground they filled with ice
from frozen ponds. People also used springhouses, similar to an icehouse
but with cold water from underground springs running through them.*

☞ *To preserve meat and fish, colonists packed them in salt,
or they "cured" pork into ham and bacon in smokehouses.
Mount Vernon was famous for its hams.*

If others talk at Table be attentive but talk not with Meat in your Mouth.

We all like to think if we're talking,
other people are listening. Just remember
not to talk with your mouth full of
anything but your teeth!

 George probably had to remind himself a lot to be attentive
and listen to other people at the table, because day after day, he sat down to eat with
guests, and a lot of them were strangers!

 In those days, you had to offer hospitality to anybody who stopped by,
and hundreds of people came to Mount Vernon to visit the famous George Washington.
Not only did these hordes of people have meals with the Washingtons, they might even spend
a few days. But however hard all those guests were on George and Martha,
the couple always did their duty.

And what was it like for kids at those fancy dinners?
Well, they weren't necessarily allowed to come, but if they did, they might have to stand at
the table instead of sit, and they were supposed to be perfect little gents and ladies.

Be not Angry at Table whatever happens & if you have reason to be so, Shew it not but {put} on a Chearfull Countenance . . .

These days, we don't always sit down to eat meals together like people did when George was around. But when we do, it's a lot better—way more fun and better for our health—to have good talks instead of bad ones!

 *Many cheerful people gathered around for those big colonial feasts. Slaves in the kitchen at Mount Vernon got up at about four in the morning to start fixing the food for the Washingtons and their guests.*

Numerous enslaved black men, women, and children worked at Mount Vernon. Most slaves worked pretty much from dawn to dusk. George said he gave his workers two hours off in the afternoons for their main meal, and they had Sundays and some holidays to themselves.

Drink not nor talk with your mouth full neither Gaze about you while you are a Drinking.

You've surely heard "Don't talk with your mouth full!"—advice that never grows old. And now that we can carry water wherever we go, we can keep our eyes from roamin' and our attention on the company we're keepin'.

☞ *So what did they drink back then? Well, not that much water, because it wasn't particularly safe. They sure didn't get their water from a tap in their kitchen, the way we do. They got it from wells and other sources.*

☞ *They also drank boiled milk (they didn't know about pasteurization yet, which makes raw milk safe to drink), apple cider, tea, and coffee. But the caffeinated delicacies had to be shipped from other countries. (Remember the Boston Tea Party?) Hot chocolate was also a popular drink, but mostly for adults, who considered it too "stimulating" for kids.*

☞ *Grown-ups also drank wine, rum, and whiskey. Mount Vernon had one of the biggest distilleries around, and the whiskey sold from it made George a lot of cash.*

In Company of your Betters be not longer in eating than they are lay not your Arm but only your hand upon the table.

It's a little awkward when your guests are ready for dessert and you're still pickin' at your peas. But it's definitely not as awkward as putting your shoulders, elbows, and arms all over the table.

☞ *The biggest meal of the day at Mount Vernon could take a long, long time— two hours or more if there was company. It was called dinner, and it was served at two or three in the afternoon.*

☞ *Sometimes George and Martha's fancy dinners had 21 dishes in the first course, then just as many in the second. Meals included all kinds of meats, poultry, and vegetables raised or grown at Mount Vernon. Plus there were oysters and fish from the Potomac River, which was practically in George's front yard. He and his friends and slaves also hunted wild ducks, geese, pigeons, deer, and other game for the dinner table. Hungry yet?*

☞ *Leave room for dessert. Pies, cakes, puddings, tarts, and candies were all part of the grand finale, with fruits and nuts at the very end.*

*P*ut not your meat to your Mouth with your *K*nife in your hand neither *S*pit forth the *S*tones of any fruit *P*ye upon a *D*ish nor *C*ast anything under the table.

It's still not a good idea to keep your knife clenched in your hand while you fork food into your mouth or to throw fruit pits or anything else under the table.

☞ *Forks weren't as common in colonial America, particularly for the poor and "middling classes" (today we say the "middle class"), so some people were "knife-eaters" and used wide knives to shovel food into their mouths.*

☞ *The gentry—rich folk—had forks but usually with just two or three prongs instead of the three or four our forks have. Polite people used forks to spear food like meat, but they might also use a fork to push softer food onto their knife then put the knife in their mouth.*

☞ *As to fruit pies, Virginians back then grew plenty of fruit— cherries, apricots, peaches, apples. Some of it they put into pies, some into jams and marmalades, and some they candied or ate plain.*

Rince not your Mouth in the Presence of Others.

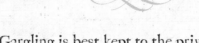

Gargling is best kept to the privacy of the bathroom, since sloshing and spitting isn't much fun to watch.

☞ *A couple of books on colonial manners warned not to spit on the floor during dinner because it was rude, so it must have been something people did back then.*

☞ *To most gentlemen or ladies in colonial America, manners were everything—and the Americans pretty much copied their manners from the British. Here's what a British earl said: "To do the Honours of a Table gracefully, is one of the outlines of a well-bred man."*

☞ *The earl also said a man should know how to do simple things like carve meat well, because if he couldn't, it would make him seem "disagreeable and ridiculous to others."*

Citiz

How to be a true-blue member of the community, friend, and overall dutiful dude

enship

When a man does all he can though it Succeeds not well blame not him that did it.

Say your buddy misses the goal in soccer or the step in ballet. They tried. They did their best. No need to blame them.

☞ The thing about G.W. is that he probably took a lot of grief from his mother when he was a boy. His father died when George was just 11, and George had to become the "man of the house."

☞ George's mother, Mary, was strict with her kids, compared to most parents today. She read to them every day from a book called Contemplations Moral and Divine. She criticized George a lot, and that likely made him tough, self-reliant, and uncomplaining.

☞ But George was also sensitive to criticism and wanted the approval of other people. He felt that his behavior needed to be almost perfect.

Strive not with your Superiers in argument, but always Submit your Judgment to others with Modesty.

In George's day, kids didn't argue with
their elders. These days, it's okay to say what
you think, as long as you show some
respect when you do it.

☞ *Since G.W. didn't have a dad when he was a young man, he looked up
to older men he admired and tried to copy their good points. He also got
them to admire him by being modest, hardworking, and that other very
important thing to Virginians—genteel and mannerly.*

☞ *George impressed some of the most important men in the colony,
including the governor and the richest landowner. But he also argued with
them during the French and Indian War over his pay and rank.*

☞ *G.W. learned this rule the hard way. People in power
usually win the argument.*

Associate yourself with Men of good Quality if you Esteem your own Reputation; for 'tis better to be alone than in bad Company.

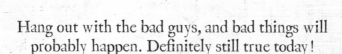

Hang out with the bad guys, and bad things will probably happen. Definitely still true today!

☞ *George was born into the haughty world of the Virginia gentry—mostly rich folks—but his family really didn't have a lot of money when he was growing up.*

☞ *He didn't get to go to college like most boys of the gentry. He taught himself to behave like a gentleman by copying how other people in "polite society" behaved and by studying the rules of civility.*

☞ *When G.W. was 26 years old, he married Martha Custis, a wealthy and respected widow in Virginia's gentry. By then he was also master of Mount Vernon, so he was definitely moving up in the world.*

Speak not Evil of the absent for it is unjust.

Don't go gossiping behind other people's backs
or sending nasty text messages about them.
Not cool.

☞ *The colonial gentry could be big gossips—even though
gossiping was actually considered a "sin"—always talking about
other people and whether their friends' behaviors,
dress, or houses were good enough.*

☞ *The rich didn't have much opportunity to gossip, though, because they
lived so spread out, on their huge plantations with just their own families
and the slaves who worked for them. Market days in town were a good
time to catch up on gossip, and so were the winter months, when friends or
relatives would stay with each other for weeks at a time.*

☞ *Some planters also had grand homes in Virginia's then capital,
Williamsburg, and they spent winter months there, entertaining each
other and going to fancy balls.*

Let your Recreations be Manfull not Sinfull.

Better to play the guitar or Frisbee,
or to go to the movies with friends, than to play
mean pranks on other people.

☞ *George was a big, athletic guy, and here's the kind of "manfull" stuff he liked to do: He loved riding horses and hunting, particularly fox hunting, a big sport in Virginia back then. He also loved to throw, and once he told an aide he could throw a stone farther than anyone he knew. He would have made a great pitcher or quarterback.*

☞ *When he was young, he liked to swim in the Rappahannock River and to fence and play billiards (a game like pool). And when he was older, he enjoyed being a farmer and taking care of his plantation.*

☞ *When he became commander of the army, he issued orders forbidding "profane cursing, swearing and drunkenness" as well as "gaming" (gambling) of every kind.*

Detract not from others neither be excessive in Commanding.

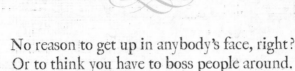

No reason to get up in anybody's face, right?
Or to think you have to boss people around.
That's never a good way to get people movin' in
the direction you want.

☞ *In old Virginia, you probably would never have seen a mother yelling at her kids like this one—at least not among George's hoity-toity crowd. And kids wouldn't have been fighting each other on the street, either.*

☞ *In early America, people really cared about acting properly, so kids had rules of behavior drilled into them. The Jesuit rules G.W. learned were just one variety. There were a lot of books on how to behave. Here's the name of a popular one:* A Companion for Young Ladies and Young Gentlemen: In Which Their Duty to God and their Parents, their Carriage to Superiors and Inferiors, and several other very useful and instructive Lessons are recommended.

In writing or Speaking, give to every Person his due Title According to his Degree & the Custom of the Place.

These days we don't typically use a lot of fancy titles, but still, it's not a good idea to say to your teacher or principal, "Hey, dude."

☞ People liked titles in George's day and used them a lot. They also had a fancier, more formal way of speaking.

☞ Once during the Revolutionary War, the enemy commander sent George a letter asking to talk to him. But the letter was addressed to "George Washington, Esq. etc., etc." instead of General Washington, so George refused to even look at it. Finally, the British officer sent him one addressed to "His Excellency, General Washington."

☞ George may have wanted the British to acknowledge his rank out of respect for America. But when the war was over and he became President, he wanted a more democratic way of doing things. G.W. preferred not to be addressed as Your Excellency—he wanted to be called Mr. President.

Speak not in an unknown Tongue in Company but in your own Language . . .

An unknown tongue in G.W.'s day meant a foreign language. Today, it could also mean "OMG," or "LOL." Okay, maybe your parents know those, but probably not the rest of your lingo.

☞ *George had a tutor, but other than that, he didn't have a lot of formal schooling or go to college, and he didn't speak any other languages well, though he may have known a little German and Latin. He may also have learned a few words of French, because he had so many friends who were French officers during the Revolution.*

☞ *Another Founding Father, Thomas Jefferson, went to the College of William & Mary in Williamsburg, Virginia, where he read Greek, Latin, French, Italian, Spanish, and English. He also traveled throughout Europe when he was an American ambassador and may have learned some German.*

☞ *G.W. never got farther from home than a trip he took when he was 19, to the Caribbean island of Barbados.*

De

Good manners, tips for talking, standing, sitting, and just looking around

corium

In the Presence of Others Sing not to yourself with a humming Noise, nor Drum with your Fingers or Feet.

Early Americans couldn't pump up the beats with headphones. But since we can, we should pay attention to this rule and not sing or drum our fingers to a tune nobody else can hear.

☞ *Like most Virginians, G.W. loved to dance. He called it an "agreeable and innocent amusement." And he paid for dance lessons when he was a young man.*

☞ *Wealthy planters like George hosted fancy balls in their own homes. Most dancing was not the free-form kind we do today but more formal.*

☞ *One young man who came to Virginia to be a tutor described how an evening might go: "About Seven the Ladies & Gentlemen beg[a]n to dance in the Ball-Room—first Minuets one Round; Second Giggs [jigs]; third Reels; And last of All Country-Dances; . . . The Music was a French-Horn and two violins—The Ladies were Dressed Gay, and splendid, & when dancing, their Silks & Brocades rustled and trailed behind them!"*

Sleep not when others Speak, Sit not when others stand, Speak not when you Should hold your Peace, walk not on when others Stop.

These days it's sometimes okay to sit
while other people stand. But sleeping when
your friends are talking? How rude!

☞ *Sleep habits were a lot different in George's life from what they are now.*
The only light people had was firelight or candlelight, since there was no electricity
to keep the night bright. So they went to bed early and got up with the sun.

☞ *But people didn't necessarily sleep straight through the night.*
Sometimes they slept till about midnight, then woke up on their own (no alarm clock)
and spent a couple of hours reading, praying, thinking, or talking.
After that, they went back to sleep till daybreak.

☞ *Some kids slept with brothers or sisters, sometimes three or four to a bed,*
depending on how poor or wealthy the family was, and how cold it was.
They might snuggle up for warmth in winter.

At Play and at Fire its Good manners to Give Place to the last Commer, and affect not to Speak Louder than Ordinary.

Even if you're a little bit late to the party, it's always nice when a friend saves you a seat. But yelling just to be heard definitely isn't okay.

☞ George was no shouter—he was a reserved man who used words carefully. When he was older, he was actually pretty deaf, probably because the roar of cannon and gunfire on the battlefield damaged his hearing.

☞ In early America, the fireplace was usually the only source of warmth, so everybody deserved a chance to stand or sit near it.

☞ Fireplaces were also really dangerous, and homes burned down much more often than they do today. In fact, when George was young, his family's house caught fire on Christmas Eve. Nobody was hurt, though.

Run not in the Streets, neither go too slowly nor with Mouth open go not Shaking yr Arms . . . go not upon the Toes, nor in a Dancing fashion.

This pretty much means: "Be cool, be calm."

☞ *George must have liked this rule, because he always made sure he looked cool, calm, and collected.*

☞ *A friend said, "His demeanor [is] at all times composed and dignified. His movement and gestures are graceful, his walk majestic."*

☞ *George also looked really good in the saddle, where he spent a lot of his time. Thomas Jefferson called him "the best horseman of his age, and the most graceful figure that could be seen on horseback."*

Shake not the head, . . . lift not one eyebrow higher than the other . . . and bedew no mans face with your Spittle, by approaching too near him when you Speak.

Now that's a lot to remember, but everybody hates to get the hairy eyeball, let alone getting "bedewed"—showered with little bits of spit from a chatty friend.

☞ *Today, we know that spit is more than just gross, it's a real germ carrier. But doctors in George's day didn't know much about how diseases spread, and a lot of people died of fevers and diarrhea caused by contagious diseases.*

☞ *Ever heard of an apothecary? That is what a pharmacist used to be called. People who had aches and pains often went to an apothecary's shop to ask how to treat their ailments. Or they might treat themselves.*

☞ *Here's one recipe they had for a homemade cold tablet: Take some pearls, crab's-eyes, red coral, white amber, burnt hartshorn, oriental bezoar, and the black tips of crab claws, and make a paste using the jelly of vipers. Then roll the paste into little balls. This wasn't very effective but some of their remedies worked.*

In visiting the Sick, do not Presently play the Physicion if you be not Knowing therein.

You probably don't want to give your friends advice on medicine. Best to leave that to the doctor or to their parents.

Medicine is always changing. As far back as the ancient Egyptians, people used leeches to suck out "bad" blood and cure everything from fevers to flatulence. And today, some doctors are using leeches again to help heal wounds!

In G.W.'s time, doctors would "bleed" people, even without leeches. In his last days, that's what George requested for himself. He had gotten chilled while he was out on his horse one day in the rain and snow. At first he was fine, but then he felt sick and could hardly breathe. He asked his doctors to "bleed" him, but nothing helped. On the night of December 14, 1799, he died in his bed at Mount Vernon.

The Gestures of the Body must be Suited to the discourse you are upon.

So, don't make goofy faces or wave your hands.
It makes you look strange and it
weirds out your friends.

☞ *Just like he paid attention to his posture and body movements, George was careful with his expressions. One of his admirers said George kept his mouth "generally firmly closed" and "all the muscles of his face under perfect control, tho flexible and expressive of deep feeling when moved by emotions." Basically, his expression was "pleasing and benevolent tho . . . commanding."*

☞ *A lot of George's soldiers said they felt less afraid and more confident when they looked at him and saw his calm expression when times were tough—which they mostly were during the Revolution.*

Play not the Peacock, looking every where about you, to See if you be well Deck't . . .

Ever heard the expression
"proud as a peacock"? That's what this rule is
all about. Skip the peacockery.

☛ *Peacocks like to strut their stuff, fanning out their big beautiful feathery tails so they can be admired. You may know people who do something like that—posing so everybody can admire how awesome they look.*

☛ *G.W. never posed like a peacock, but he did have one at Mount Vernon. A lot of colonial plantations had peafowl strutting and screeching around their gardens. G.W. and Martha also liked parrots and kept them in cages.*

☛ *Everybody who knew George said he was a very modest man. Someone even said he was "if anything too modest." The only time G.W. may not have been very modest was when he was young and serving with the British in the French and Indian War. He kept pushing to be promoted. But lots of young people are really ambitious, so we won't hold that against him.*

Gaze not on the marks or blemishes of Others and ask not how they came.

Nobody likes to be stared at or made fun
of for blemishes, scars, or other stuff that makes
them feel weird about their looks.

☞ *Smallpox caused lots of scars in G.W.'s day.
Even before his time, it was a killer disease. Smallpox causes fever,
aches, pains, and a horrible blistery rash.*

☞ *Queen Elizabeth I, who ruled England about 130 years before
George was born, had bad scars from smallpox. She wore a lot of ghostly
white powder to cover them up. When G.W. was a young man, he got
smallpox himself on his trip to Barbados. But he had a mild
case that left only a few scars.*

☞ *The only people who liked their smallpox scars were pirates,
because the scars made them look more ferocious.*

Hy

Habits to keep you
clean, healthy, and
snazzy

giene

When in Company, put not your Hands to any Part of the Body, not usualy Discovered.

No scrounging under the armpits, in the nose,
or in other out-of-sight places.

☞ *Early Americans took this rule a lot further, especially the girls.*
Young ladies were supposed to keep their hands in their laps or keep them busy with
embroidery and learning to play musical instruments. Men and older boys were
supposed to sit up straight and maybe rest their fists on their thighs.

☞ *As for rummaging in the nose, there are ancient cave paintings that seem to show*
men and women with their fingers lodged in a nostril.

☞ *Today, doctors actually have a big word for compulsive nose-picking.*
They call it rhinotillexomania.

If You Cough, Sneeze, Sigh, or Yawn, do it not Loud but Privately, ... but put Your handkercheif or Hand before your face and turn aside.

Don't sneeze or cough into the air but into the crook of your arm, and keep a tissue handy. And it's always polite to cover your mouth when yawning.

☞ Since early Americans didn't understand that diseases were contagious, they probably wouldn't have put this rule under hygiene.

☞ People could be very superstitious back then. Some even thought witches could put a curse on you and make you sick!

☞ Science was a new way to understand the world in G.W.'s day. Remember Sir Isaac Newton and his falling apple and gravity? Well, he died just before G.W. was born, and he was sort of the father of modern science. Of course, you know who the big celebrity scientist and inventor in America was at that time? That's right, Benjamin Franklin. His experiments with electricity made him a superstar, even in Europe.

Put not off your Cloths in the presence of Others, nor go out your Chamber half Drest.

It's still a good idea not to wear clothes that
make you seem half-dressed or to "put off your
clothes" in front of other people.

☞ *They had some funny notions in G.W.'s time. Ladies wore long skirts and
some kind of head covering whenever they left the house, but they might also
wear very low-cut dresses for special occasions.*

☞ *George knew that dress mattered. Like the rest of the colonial gentry, he
ordered his clothes from Britain. They were custom-made for him,
so he could order exactly what he wanted.*

☞ *When the Americans and British began fighting over taxes just
before the Revolution, Americans stopped trading as much with Britain.
Instead, they started spinning and weaving cloth called "homespun."
Wearing clothes made out of homespun meant you were a real patriot.*

Shift not yourself in the Sight of others nor Gnaw your nails.

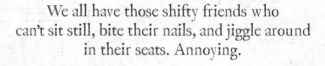

We all have those shifty friends who can't sit still, bite their nails, and jiggle around in their seats. Annoying.

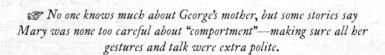

☞ *No one knows much about George's mother, but some stories say Mary was none too careful about "comportment"—making sure all her gestures and talk were extra polite.*

☞ *Some historians don't think Mary's mother could read or write. By the time Mary was 12, she was an orphan, so family friends took her in. That happened a lot in early America, when life was rough and people died young.*

☞ *Legend has it that Mary may even have smoked a pipe, or who knows, gnawed her nails! We'll never really know the truth about Mary, but she doesn't seem to have taught G.W. the finer things. He had to learn them on his own.*

Kill no Vermin as Fleas, lice ticks &c in the Sight of Others . . . if it be upon the Cloths of your Companions, Put it off privately . . .

We still don't like lice and ticks, but we do like
to get them off of us as quickly as possible.

☞ Lice were an even bigger problem in colonial times than now. Not just head lice but body lice, too. That's because people often crowded into close spaces. If you traveled, there weren't any real hotels, just simple inns. If you stayed in one, you might have to share a bed with a stranger—or two—a good way to get "vermin."

☞ Ships that brought people from Europe to America were like lice rafts. One man wrote that "the lice abound so frightfully, especially on sick people, that they can be scraped off the body."

☞ There were lots of lotions and potions for lice. In fact, Benjamin Franklin's mother-in-law made one that Ben advertised for sale as Widow Read's Ointment.

Keep your Nails clean and Short, also your Hands and Teeth Clean yet without Shewing any great Concern for them.

Don't pick at your hands, fingernails, or teeth in
public. Clean them up in private.

☞ *If you think about it, keeping his hands and nails clean wouldn't have
been that easy for George. Almost every job he had kept him outdoors, not
the best way to have lily-white hands and perfect nails.*

☞ *Here are all the positions he held over his lifetime: soldier twice
(in the French and Indian War and the Revolution); surveyor working on
the Virginia frontier; owner of Mount Vernon, where he oversaw the
farm and fished and rode; and President.*

Wear not your Cloths, foul, unript or Dusty but See they be Brush'd once every day at least and take heed that you approach not to any Uncleaness.

No need to go all out, just wear clean clothes.
Wonder what G.W. would think of the faded,
worn jeans and T-shirt look.

☞ Notice how the rule says to "see they be brush'd"? It doesn't say to "brush them." That's because the gentry class had servants to brush and clean their clothes for them.

☞ Rich girls and boys in the South even had their own personal slaves, kids about their own age who took care of them and were sometimes their friends. When George was 11 and his father died, he inherited ten slaves. But his mother gave them their orders.

☞ One of G.W.'s most faithful servants was a slave named Billy Lee. Besides taking care of George's clothes and serving as his waiter, Billy entertained him with stories and was about as good a horseman as his "master." He was with G.W. all through the Revolution.

Co

Best ways to show some respect to your buds, your teachers, and your parents

urtesy

Shew Nothing to your Freind that may affright him.

Don't jump out of a dark hallway in front of
your little brother or put a fake snake under
your friend's pillow at camp. Being scary is just
never going to get you very far!

☞ G.W. tried not to "affright" his soldiers during the Revolution by
telling them how bad things were. But he was plenty worried himself.

☞ The first year of the war, he wrote to a friend:
"The reflection upon my situation and that of this army produces
many an uneasy hour when all around me are wrapped in sleep.
Few people know the predicament we are in."

☞ Instead of telling his men that their army, and America, was in
serious trouble, George kept telling them they needed to stay and fight for
liberty and freedom. And most of those tired, dirty, hungry soldiers stayed
because they believed in George Washington.

When you meet with one of Greater Quality than yourself, Stop, and retire especially if it be at a Door or any Straight place to give way for him to Pass.

We aren't as polite as all that now, but we still wouldn't leap in front of Grandma so we can get through the door first or butt in front of the principal in the cafeteria line.

☞ *The colonials were all about social rank. When they threw a big dinner and it was time to sit down, the hostess would ask the most important female guest to lead the way into the dining room, followed by the second most important, then the third, and so on.*

☞ *The hostess was the last lady in line, then the gentlemen would line up by rank. And guess what—they all had seat assignments based on that same lineup.*

☞ *One manners book warned, "Nothing is considered as a greater mark of ill-breeding, than for a person to interrupt this order, or seat himself higher than he ought." Talk about knowing your place!*

Undertake not to Teach your equal in the art himself Proffesses; it Savours of arrogancy.

It's still annoying when somebody tries to tell
you how to do something when you know how
to do it as well as they do.

☞ *There was one time in his life when G.W. acted pretty arrogant:
When the Revolution first started, there really wasn't an army,
just New Englanders who had trained themselves to be soldiers. G.W.
was not impressed and judged them by snobby Virginia gentry standards.*

☞ *They may not have been fancy, but those New England boys
could fight. They had already taken on the British, the best army in the
world, at Lexington, Concord, and Bunker Hill. And G.W. realized soon
enough how brave they were. He encouraged his army to read and study to
become even better soldiers.*

Use no Reproachfull Language against any one neither Curse nor Revile.

If you've got a beef with somebody,
don't let your temper take over your words.

☞ *G.W. definitely wanted to be a chill guy who never cussed anybody out. But a few times during the Revolution he lost his temper in a big way.*

☞ *One time was in 1776 in New York City, when his troops ran away from the British in a fight. He completely lost it, shouting at his men, throwing his hat on the ground, and yelling, "Good God! Have I got such troops as these?"*

☞ *Everybody who knew George well knew that he had a temper. But they also knew that he tried hard to keep it under control. And most of the time, he did.*

While you are talking, Point not with your Finger at him of Whom you Discourse nor Approach too near him to whom you talk especially to his face.

None of us like to have a know-it-all
shake a finger in our face and tell us what's
what. Bossy, bossy, bossy.

☞ *G.W. had a thing about people getting too close and touching him. He didn't like it, and that could have been a problem with his French allies in the Revolution.*

☞ *His favorite French officer, the Marquis de Lafayette, would give G.W. a great big squeeze when they'd reunite. Another Frenchman, an admiral, once gave him a huge hug and kisses on both cheeks and called him "my dear small general."*

☞ *That was a joke, of course, because G.W. was about 6 feet 2 inches (1.9 m) tall. The admiral was only a couple of inches taller than that!*

Let your Discourse with Men of Business be Short and Comprehensive.

Keep your business messages short and sweet and to the point. (George would have liked tweeting 'cause it makes you do that.)

☞ *George was a huge writer—he wrote many thousands of letters, orders, and other papers in his lifetime. Even during the Revolutionary War, after a day of battle, he would sit down and write at night.*

☞ *He was careful in his letter writing, saying exactly what he needed to but not rambling on and on about stuff that didn't matter.*

☞ *He knew all those papers were important so he took good care of them, saving the ones he got and making copies of the letters he sent out. After he died, though, his papers got scattered to different places and some were lost. But there are still enough left to fill volumes.*

Turn not your Back to others especially in Speaking, Jog not the Table or Desk on which Another reads or writes, lean not upon any one.

Well, maybe leaning a little on the guy
or girl next to you is okay these days, if the leaned-on doesn't
mind, but nobody likes table-joggers or friends who turn
away when they're speaking to you.

☞ *Americans back in the 1700s weren't typing away on laptops.*
They were writing everything in cursive and using pens. And not tidy ballpoints.
They were using quill pens, made of feathers plucked from live birds.

☞ *Goose feathers were fine; swan feathers were better, but swans can be even nastier*
than geese when you try to get near them. The feathers had to be buried in hot, dry sand to
harden the pointy ends, called nibs. Then the nibs were cut with a penknife.

☞ *To write, you would dip the nib in ink and scribble, scribble, scribble.*
Good penmanship was important to the early Americans, but when the nib got dull,
ink would drip from it and make a mess. And what a bummer if somebody jogged
the table while you were scribbling!

Be not froward but friendly and Courteous; the first to Salute hear and answer & be not Pensive when it's a time to Converse.

Being "froward" meant being stubborn. And being courteous was epic for G.W. and his Virginia clan.

☞ Did Virginians kill with kindness? A young tutor who came to Virginia wrote, "Virginians are so kind one can scarce know how to dispense with, or indeed accept their kindness."

☞ Each of the 13 Colonies had their own style and way of doing things. In Pennsylvania, a colony settled by Quakers, a lot of people used "thee" and "thou" instead of "you," and they believed in being simple in their tastes.

☞ In Massachusetts, where many Puritans settled, people believed in being "pensive." They were all about education. In fact, they founded the first college in America—Harvard—in 1636. The second, Virginia's William & Mary, wasn't founded until 1693.

When Another Speaks be attentive your Self and disturb not the Audience . . . Interrupt him not, nor Answer him till his Speech be ended.

It's always a good thing to let the
other guy have his say, instead of jumping in
and interrupting.

☞ *George could certainly keep his mouth shut and listen. In a lot of ways,
his quietness made him powerful. It probably also helped make him President.*

☞ *While everybody else was yelling and arguing with each other over
what kind of laws the new country should have, G.W. sat in dignified silence as
President of the Constitutional Convention. When he did speak, people
knew it was something important.*

☞ *He kept his cool, too, for the next eight years, as the first President of the
United States, even though arguing, interrupting, and bickering went on among the
other Founding Fathers. But George's cool kept them all a little cooler,
and the new country a little more solid.*

Int

How to be righteous and awesome, like George himself was

egrity

Be no Flatterer, neither Play with any that delights not to be Play'd Withal.

This probably means a fake flatterer,
because there's nothing wrong with dishin' out
a compliment here and there when you mean it.

☞ *George probably used some flattery on the ladies, because he liked them. Before he married Martha, he fell pretty hard for a few girls, but they were part of the rich gentry and out of his league. He didn't have much going for him yet, so he was hardly a catch.*

☞ *During the French and Indian War, he became a hero. He moved to Mount Vernon and was making it a fine place. That's when he met Martha.*

☞ *Martha and George had a good marriage, but it wasn't an easy or happy time for America. They were there for each other, however, during all the years of war and nation building.*

Shew not yourself glad at the Misfortune of another though he were your enemy.

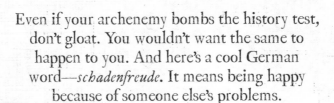

Even if your archenemy bombs the history test, don't gloat. You wouldn't want the same to happen to you. And here's a cool German word—*schadenfreude*. It means being happy because of someone else's problems.

☞ *G.W. sure could have acted that way at the end of the Revolutionary War. The big, bad enemy, Britain, had lost the war to little old America. He could have gloated, particularly in front of the commander who lost the final battle at Yorktown, Virginia.*

☞ *That guy, Lord Cornwallis, was so upset at losing the battle that he wouldn't even come to the surrender ceremony. George, perfect gent that he was, still invited Cornwallis to a dinner party he threw for the officers who had fought on all sides of the war.*

☞ *Cornwallis didn't come to that, either. But the next day, he went to see Washington, and the two commanders rode through the battlefield together—a final farewell to the war.*

Undertake not what you cannot perform but be carefull to keep your promise.

Have you ever said you'd do something
that you were pretty sure you couldn't? Or promised
more than you thought you could deliver?

George actually didn't think he was up to being commander in chief of the Continental Army when he was first asked to do it in 1775. He wrote this worried letter to Martha (he called her Patcy): "Far from seeking this appointment I have used every endeavour in my power to avoid it . . . its being a trust too far great for my Capacity." But George also said that "destiny" had "thrown me upon this Service." So he took the job.

Six long, hard years later, when the British were finally beaten, G.W. wrote to Congress and said, "I consider myself to have done only my duty and in the execution of that, I ever feel myself happy." Two more years would pass before the Treaty of Paris officially ended the Revolutionary War.

Let your Conversation be without Malice or Envy, for 'tis a Sign of a Tractable and Commendable Nature . . .

This is another one of those "chill" rules—keep your head, don't act jealous or nasty. Try to be reasonable instead of emotional when you get riled up.

 *John Adams, another Founding Father, could have learned a thing or two from this rule. He was a smart man, a lawyer from Massachusetts, but he was also really envious and resented the attention other Founding Fathers got.*

 *John A. said or wrote some mean things about Thomas Jefferson, Ben Franklin, G.W., and almost everybody else. He once even said that George was "too illiterate, unlearned, unread for his station and reputation."*

 *Apparently, other Americans didn't think that, because G.W. was elected President twice and could have kept serving until he died if he hadn't stepped down himself. John A. was in fact President right after George, but he wasn't reelected to a second term.*

Be not immodest in urging your Freinds to Discover a Secret.

We all have secrets that we don't
want people prying into, so we shouldn't
pry into other people's.

☞ G.W. belonged to an ancient secret society, or fraternity, called the
Masons. A lot of important Americans back then were also Masons,
including Ben Franklin.

☞ G.W. laid the cornerstone of the U.S. Capitol in a Masonic ceremony.
He wore his Masonic sash and embroidered apron, and he put corn, wine,
and oil on the cornerstone while other Masons stood nearby.

☞ The Masons are still around and their exact beliefs are still
pretty secret. They don't like anyone poking around trying to discover their
mysteries. But they also do a lot of charitable work to help people, whether
those people are Masons or not.

Be not hasty to beleive flying Reports to the Disparagement of any.

These days, rumors fly thick and fast everywhere—
especially online, through text messages, and on
social networks like Facebook. Don't believe
everything you hear and don't pass along rumors.
Next time they could be aimed at you.

☞ *When G.W. left the Presidency and it was time to elect a new leader, things got pretty crazy. It was the first real campaign, and John Adams and Thomas Jefferson were the big contenders. The rumors started to fly.*

☞ *John's side called Tom "a mean-spirited, low-lived fellow, the son of a half-breed Indian squaw." Tom's side called John a tyrant, a fool, and a criminal.*

☞ *In the end, John won, but here's the funny thing: When they were old men, John and Tom became best buds, writing long letters to each other. They even died on the same day, July 4, 1826, exactly 50 years after the Declaration of Independence was signed.*

Labour to keep alive in your Breast that Little Spark of Celestial fire Called Conscience.

Having a conscience that keeps you honest and fair is as good an idea now as it was in George's day. So here's to that little spark called conscience!

☞ *Slavery bothered George's conscience, even though he owned lots of slaves, and they did most of the work at Mount Vernon. In his will, he said they should be freed after Martha died. But Martha didn't wait that long. About a year after George died, she freed them herself.*

☞ *Almost two centuries after G.W. died, someone put together a book called* Maxims of George Washington—*things he said or wrote that were, well, rules to live by. Here's one maxim he wrote after all his long years of service to his country: "Without Virtue and without integrity the finest talents and the most brilliant accomplishments can never gain respect." Now that's a rule to remember and live by!*

1st Every Action done in Company, ought to be with Some Sign of Respect, to those that are Present.

2d When in Company, put not your Hands to any Part of the Body, not usualy Discovered.

3d Shew Nothing to your Freind that may affright him.

4th In the Presence of Others Sing not to yourself with a humming Noise, nor Drum with your Fingers or Feet.

5th If You Cough, Sneeze, Sigh, or Yawn, do it not Loud but Privately; and Speak not in your Yawning, but put Your handkercheif or Hand before your face and turn aside.

6th Sleep not when others Speak, Sit not when others stand, Speak not when you Should hold your Peace, walk not on when others Stop.

7th Put not off your Cloths in the presence of Others, nor go out your Chamber half Drest.

8th At Play and at Fire its Good manners to Give Place to the last Commer, and affect not to Speak Louder than Ordinary.

9th Spit not in the Fire, nor Stoop low before it neither Put your Hands into the Flames to warm them, nor Set your Feet upon the Fire especially if there be meat before it.

10th When you Sit down, Keep your Feet firm and Even, without putting one on the other or Crossing them.

11th Shift not yourself in the Sight of others nor Gnaw your nails.

12th Shake not the head, Feet, or Legs rowl not the Eys lift not one eyebrow higher than the other wry not the mouth, and bedew no mans face with your Spittle, by approaching too near him when you Speak.

13th Kill no Vermin as Fleas, lice ticks &c in the Sight of Others, if you See any filth or thick Spittle put your foot Dexteriously upon it if it be upon the Cloths of your Companions, Put it off privately, and if it be upon your own Cloths return Thanks to him who puts it off.

14th Turn not your Back to others especially in Speaking, Jog not the Table or Desk on which Another reads or writes, lean not upon any one.

15th Keep your Nails clean and Short, also your Hands and Teeth Clean yet without Shewing any great Concern for them.

16th Do not Puff up the Cheeks, Loll not out the tongue rub the Hands, or beard, thrust out the lips, or bite them or keep the Lips too open or too Close.

17th Be no Flatterer, neither Play with any that delights not to be Play'd Withal.

18th Read no Letters, Books, or Papers in Company but when there is a Necessity for the doing of it you must ask leave: come not near the Books or Writings of Another so as to read them unless desired or give your opinion of them unask'd also look not nigh when another is writing a Letter.

19th Let your Countenance be pleasant but in Serious Matters Somewhat grave.

20th The Gestures of the Body must be Suited to the discourse you are upon.

21st Reproach none for the Infirmaties of Nature, nor Delight to Put them that have in mind thereof.

22d Shew not yourself glad at the Misfortune of another though he were your enemy.

23d When you see a Crime punished, you may be inwardly Pleased; but always shew Pity to the Suffering Offender.

24th Do not laugh too loud or too much at any Publick Spectacle.

25th Superfluous Complements and all Affectation of Ceremonie are to be avoided, yet where due they are not to be Neglected.

26th In Pulling off your Hat to Persons of Distinction, as Noblemen, Justices, Churchmen &c make a Reverence, bowing more or less according to the Custom of the Better Bred, and Quality of the Person. Amongst your equals expect not always that they Should begin with you first, but to Pull off the Hat when there is no need is Affectation, in the Manner of Saluting and resaluting in words keep to the most usual Custom.

27th Tis ill manners to bid one more eminent than yourself be covered as well as not to do it to whom it's due Likewise he that makes too much haste to Put on his hat does not well, yet he ought to Put it on at the first, or at most the Second time of being ask'd; now what is herein

Spoken, of Qualification in behaviour in Saluting, ought also to be observed in taking of Place, and Sitting down for ceremonies without Bounds is troublesome.

28th If any one come to Speak to you while you are are Sitting Stand up tho he be your Inferiour, and when you Present Seats let it be to every one according to his Degree.

29th When you meet with one of Greater Quality than yourself, Stop, and retire especially if it be at a Door or any Straight place to give way for him to Pass.

30th In walking the highest Place in most Countrys Seems to be on the right hand therefore Place yourself on the left of him whom you desire to Honour: but if three walk together the middest Place is the most Honourable the wall is usually given to the most worthy if two walk together.

31st If any one far Surpasses others, either in age, Estate, or Merit yet would give Place to a meaner than himself in his own lodging or elsewhere the one ought not to except it, So he on the other part should not use much earnestness nor offer it above once or twice.

32d To one that is your equal, or not much inferior you are to give the cheif Place in your Lodging and he to who 'tis offered ought at the first to refuse it but at the Second to accept though not without acknowledging his own unworthiness.

33d They that are in Dignity or in office have in all places Preceedency but whilst they are Young they ought to respect those that are their equals in Birth or other Qualitys, though they have no Publick charge.

34th It is good Manners to prefer them to whom we Speak before ourselves especially if they be above us with whom in no Sort we ought to begin.

35th Let your Discourse with Men of Business be Short and Comprehensive.

36th Artificers & Persons of low Degree ought not to use many ceremonies to Lords, or Others of high Degree but Respect and highly Honour them, and those of high Degree ought to treat them with affibility & Courtesie, without Arrogancy.

37th In Speaking to men of Quality do not lean nor Look them full in the Face, nor approach too near them at lest Keep a full Pace from them.

38th In visiting the Sick, do not Presently play the Physicion if you be not Knowing therein.

39th In writing or Speaking, give to every Person his due Title According to his Degree & the Custom of the Place.

40th Strive not with your Superiers in argument, but always Submit your Judgment to others with Modesty.

41st Undertake not to Teach your equal in the art himself Proffesses; it Savours of arrogancy.

42d Let thy ceremonies in Courtesie be proper to the Dignity of his place with whom thou conversest for it is absurd to act the same with a Clown and a Prince.

43d Do not express Joy before one sick or in pain for that contrary Passion will aggravate his Misery.

44th When a man does all he can though it Succeeds not well blame not him that did it.

45th Being to advise or reprehend any one, consider whether it ought to be in publick or in Private; presently, or at Some other time in what terms to do it & in reproving Shew no Sign of Cholar but do it with all Sweetness and Mildness.

46th Take all Admonitions thankfully in what Time or Place Soever given but afterwards not being culpable take a Time & Place convenient to let him him know it that gave them.

47th Mock not nor Jest at any thing of Importance break no Jest that are Sharp Biting and if you Deliver any thing witty and Pleasent abstain from Laughing there at yourself.

48th Wherein wherein you reprove Another be unblameable yourself; for example is more prevalent than Precepts.

49th Use no Reproachfull Language against any one neither Curse nor Revile.

50th Be not hasty to beleive flying Reports to the Disparagement of any.

51st Wear not your Cloths, foul, unript or Dusty but See they be Brush'd once every day at least and take heed that you approach not to any Uncleaness.

52d In your Apparel be Modest and endeavour to accomodate Nature, rather than to procure Admiration keep to the Fashion of your equals Such as are Civil and orderly with respect to Times and Places.

53d Run not in the Streets, neither go too slowly nor with Mouth open go not Shaking yr Arms kick not the earth with yr feet, go not upon the Toes, nor in a Dancing fashion.

54th Play not the Peacock, looking every where about you, to See if you be well Deck't, if your Shoes fit well if your Stokings sit neatly, and Cloths handsomely.

55th Eat not in the Streets, nor in the House, out of Season.

56th Associate yourself with Men of good Quality if you Esteem your own Reputation; for 'tis better to be alone than in bad Company.

57th In walking up and Down in a House, only with One in Company if he be Greater than yourself, at the first give him the Right hand and Stop not till he does and be not the first that turns, and when you do turn let it be with your face towards him, if he be a Man of Great Quality, walk not with him Cheek by Joul but Somewhat behind him; but yet in Such a Manner that he may easily Speak to you.

58th Let your Conversation be without Malice or Envy, for 'tis a Sign of a Tractable and Commendable Nature: And in all Causes of Passion admit Reason to Govern.

59th Never express anything unbecoming, nor Act agst the Rules Moral before your inferiours.

60th Be not immodest in urging your Freinds to Discover a Secret.

61st Utter not base and frivilous things amongst grave and Learn'd Men nor very Difficult Questians or Subjects, among the Ignorant or things hard to be believed, Stuff not your Dis-

course with Sentences amongst your Betters nor Equals.

62d Speak not of doleful Things in a Time of Mirth or at the Table; Speak not of Melancholy Things as Death and Wounds, and if others Mention them Change if you can the Discourse tell not your Dreams, but to your intimate Friend.

63d A Man ought not to value himself of his Atchievements, or rare Qualities of wit; much less of his riches Virtue or Kindred.

64th Break not a Jest where none take pleasure in mirth Laugh not aloud, nor at all without Occasion, deride no mans Misfortune, tho' there Seem to be Some cause.

65th Speak not injurious Words neither in Jest nor Earnest Scoff at none although they give Occasion.

66th Be not froward but friendly and Courteous; the first to Salute hear and answer & be not Pensive when it's a time to Converse.

67th Detract not from others neither be excessive in Commanding.

68th Go not thither, where you know not, whether you Shall be Welcome or not. Give not Advice without being Ask'd & when desired do it briefly.

69th If two contend together take not the part of either unconstrained; and be not obstinate in your own Opinion, in Things indiferent be of the Major Side.

70th Reprehend not the imperfections of others for that belongs to Parents Masters and Superiours.

71st Gaze not on the marks or blemishes of Others and ask not how they came. What you may Speak in Secret to your Friend deliver not before others.

72d Speak not in an unknown Tongue in Company but in your own Language and that as those of Quality do and not as the Vulgar; Sublime matters treat Seriously.

73d Think before you Speak pronounce not imperfectly nor bring out your Words too hastily but orderly & distinctly.

74th When Another Speaks be attentive your Self and disturb not the Audience if any hesitate in his Words help him not nor Prompt him without desired, Interrupt him not, nor Answer him till his Speech be ended.

75th In the midst of Discourse ask not of what one treateth but if you Perceive any Stop because of your coming you may well intreat him gently to Proceed: If a Person of Quality comes in while your Conversing it's handsome to Repeat what was said before.

76th While you are talking, Point not with your Finger at him of Whom you Discourse nor Approach too near him to whom you talk especially to his face.

77th Treat with men at fit Times about Business & Whisper not in the Company of Others.

78th Make no Comparisons and if any of the Company be Commended for any brave act of Vertue, commend not another for the Same.

79th Be not apt to relate News if you know not the truth thereof. In Discoursing of things you Have heard Name not your Author always A Secret Discover not.

80th Be not Tedious in Discourse or in reading unless you find the Company pleased therewith.

81st Be not Curious to Know the Affairs of Others neither approach those that Speak in Private.

82d Undertake not what you cannot perform but be carefull to keep your promise.

83d When you deliver a matter do it without passion & with discretion, however mean the person be you do it too.

84th When your Superiours talk to any Body hearken not neither Speak nor Laugh.

85th In Company of these of Higher Quality than yourself Speak not til you are ask'd a Question then Stand upright put of your Hat & Answer in few words.

86th In Disputes, be not So Desireous to Overcome as not to give Liberty to each one to deliver his Opinion and Submit to the Judgment of the Major Part especially if they are Judges of the Dispute.

87th Let thy carriage be such as becomes a Man Grave Settled and attentive to that which is spoken. Contradict not at every turn what others Say.

88th Be not tedious in Discourse, make not many Digressigns, nor repeat often the Same manner of Discourse.

89th Speak not Evil of the absent for it is unjust.

90th Being Set at meat Scratch not neither Spit Cough or blow your Nose except there's a Necessity for it.

91st Make no Shew of taking great Delight in your Victuals, Feed not with Greediness; cut your Bread with a Knife, lean not on the Table neither find fault with what you Eat.

92d Take no Salt or cut Bread with your Knife Greasy.

93d Entertaining any one at table it is decent to present him wt. meat, Undertake not to help others undesired by the Master.

94th If you Soak bread in the Sauce let it be no more than what you put in your Mouth at a time and blow not your broth at Table but Stay till Cools of it Self.

95th Put not your meat to your Mouth with your Knife in your hand neither Spit forth the Stones of any fruit Pye upon a Dish nor Cast anything under the table.

96th It's unbecoming to Stoop much to ones Meat Keep your Fingers clean & when foul wipe them on a Corner of your Table Napkin.

97th Put not another bit into your Mouth til the former be Swallowed let not your Morsels be too big for the Gowls.

98th Drink not nor talk with your mouth full neither Gaze about you while you are a Drinking.

99th Drink not too leisurely nor yet too hastily. Before and after Drinking wipe your Lips breath not then or Ever with too Great a Noise, for its uncivil.

100th Cleanse not your teeth with the Table Cloth Napkin Fork or Knife but if Others do it let it be done wt. a Pick Tooth.

101st Rince not your Mouth in the Presence of Others.

102d It is out of use to call upon the Company often to Eat nor need you Drink to others every Time you Drink.

103d In Company of your Betters be not longer in eating than they are lay not your Arm but only your hand upon the table.

104th It belongs to the Chiefest in Company to unfold his Napkin and fall to Meat first, But he ought then to Begin in time & to Dispatch with Dexterity that the Slowest may have time allowed him.

105th Be not Angry at Table whatever happens & if you have reason to be so, Shew it not but on a Chearfull Countenance especially if there be Strangers for Good Humour makes one Dish of Meat a Feast.

106th Set not yourself at the upper of the Table but if it Be your Due or that the Master of the house will have it So, Contend not, least you Should Trouble the Company.

107th If others talk at Table be attentive but talk not with Meat in your Mouth.

108th When you Speak of God or his Atributes, let it be Seriously & wt. Reverence. Honour & Obey your Natural Parents altho they be Poor.

109th Let your Recreations be Manfull not Sinfull.

110th Labour to keep alive in your Breast that Little Spark of Celestial fire Called Conscience.

Finis

☞ Acknowledgments ☜

My deepest thanks to the Colonial Williamsburg Foundation
and particularly to Cathy Hellier for her unstinting generosity in sharing the knowledge gleaned
through years of scholarship; to Paul Aron, who perpetually works to keep history alive and in
print; to Mark Hutter for lending his expertise and enthusiasm to this project;
and to the staff of the Rockefeller Library.

Appreciative thanks as well to Mount Vernon's Mary V. Thompson, who steered me unerringly in
my research, and to Mark Santangelo and the rest of his staff at the Mount Vernon library.
To Eamon and Charlotte Dougherty for their lexical consultations and for general inspiration.
And finally to my colleagues at National Geographic—Jennifer Emmett, David M. Seager, and
Kate Olesin—for the support and vision that made this project possible.   —K. M. K.

☞ Research Notes ☜

Selected Bibliography

Christmas in Williamsburg: 300 Years of Family Traditions. K. M. Kostyal, Colonial Williamsburg Foundation, National Geographic Children's Books, 2011.

Colonial Virginia's Cooking Dynasty. Katharine E. Harbury, University of South Carolina Press, 2004.

The Complete Colonial Gentleman: Cultural Legitimacy in Plantation America. Michael Jan Rozbicki, University of Virginia Press, 2003.

Dining With the Washingtons: Historic Recipes, Entertaining, and Hospitality from Mount Vernon. Ed. Stephen A. McLeod, Mount Vernon Ladies' Association, 2011.

Food. Audrey Noël Hume, Colonial Williamsburg Foundation, 1978.

Journal and Letters of Philip Vickers Fithian, 1773–1774. Ed. Hunter Dickinson Farish, University of Virginia Press, 1978.

Maxims of Washington: Political, Social, Moral, and Religious. Ed. John Frederick Schroeder, Mount Vernon Ladies' Association, 1942.

Washington: A Life. Ron Chernow, Penguin Press, 2010.

Online Sources

Colonial Williamsburg's online research site has information on etiquette, manners, and customs during the 18th century. *www.history.org*

Mount Vernon's online encyclopedia is a good place to learn more about life at Washington's home on the Potomac. *www.mountvernon .org/encyclopedia*

Some of George Washington's letters, orders to his troops, speeches, and other papers are available at these websites: *gwpapers.virginia.edu memory.loc.gov/ammem/ gwhtml/gwhome.html avalon.law.yale.edu/subject_ menus/washpap.asp*

For more background on the Rules of Civility in particular, go to *gwpapers .virginia.edu/documents/ civility/index.html*

For more on how the rules affected George's behavior, read "George Washington's 'Unmannerly Behavior': The Clash Between Civility and Honor," by William Guthrie Sayen, available online at *chnm.gmu.edu/courses/hen riques/hist615/sayen1.htm*

Thomas Jefferson's home, Monticello, also has a website that you can search for information about his life and the workings of his plantation. *www.monticello.org/site/ research-and-collections*

K. M. Kostyal has sharpened her quill pen many times to write about history and the heroics of people living through war. Her recent books include *Radical Lincoln: Inside the Mind of America's Most Fascinating President; Founding Fathers: The Fight for Freedom and the Birth of America; Christmas in Willamsburg: 300 Years of Family Traditions;* and *1776: A New Look at Revolutionary Williamsburg.* Her book *Abraham Lincoln's Extraordinary Era* was the official bicentennial book of the Abraham Lincoln Presidential Library and Museum.

Fred Harper started his career at age 19 by drawing caricatures at an amusement park in Sandusky, Ohio. After graduating from Columbus College of Art and Design, he got his pencil in the door at Marvel comics, painting posters, pinups, and covers as well as drawing interiors for Conan, Spiderman, and Doctor Strange.

Fred's work is in the private collections of the rich and powerful—but not people as cool as George Washington. His illustrations have appeared in such great publications as *Time,* the *Wall Street Journal,* the *New York Times,* the *Village Voice, Sports Illustrated,* and just about every issue of *The Week* magazine.

George Washington's
MOUNT VERNON

Since 1860, more than 85 million visitors have made George Washington's Mount Vernon the most popular historic home in America. Through thought-provoking tours, entertaining events, and stimulating educational programs on the Estate and in classrooms across the nation, Mount Vernon strives to preserve George Washington's place in history as "First in War, First in Peace, and First in the Hearts of His Countrymen." Mount Vernon is owned and operated by the Mount Vernon Ladies' Association, America's oldest national preservation organization, founded in 1853. A picturesque drive to the southern end of the George Washington Memorial Parkway, Mount Vernon is located just 16 miles from the nation's capital.

Colonial Williamsburg

The Colonial Williamsburg Foundation is a private, not-for-profit educational institution that operates the world's largest living history museum—the restored 18th-century capital of Virginia. The 301-acre "Revolutionary City" includes hundreds of restored, reconstructed, and historically furnished buildings. Costumed interpreters and tradespeople present the 18th-century world of home, politics, and work.